Case Studies in Higher Education Leadership and Management:
An Instructional Tool

D1468517

Case Studies in Higher Education Leadership and Management: An Instructional Tool

The Warner School of Education

in partnership with

the Warner Center

at

the University of Rochester

Andrew F. Wall, Ph.D. &
Chelsea BaileyShea, Ph.D., Editors

Introduction

The contemporary higher education landscape is fraught with leadership and management challenges that higher education administration graduate programs are designed to prepare current and future leaders to address. This collection of case studies grows out of the instructional challenge of creating learning experiences to meaningfully equip students with leadership and management theoretical knowledge that will guide their future practice. The cases included in this book are fictional, but they emerge from the experiences and settings of their authors. The situations found in this book are intended to cover a broad array of the type of leadership challenges that individuals at different levels of higher education might face, and would therefore need to be equipped to handle.

The majority of the case studies in this compilation emerged from a course assessment for a graduate higher education leadership and management class at the University of Rochester Warner School of Education in the spring of 2009. The assessment was aimed at gathering information that could improve the course and students' learning outcomes. The findings from the assessment exercise indicated that students desired tangible ways to apply theory to practice, and to practice leadership. A non-fruitful search for an appropriate book of case studies led to the idea of creating our own, to facilitate the active and applied teaching case study strategy. In the spring of 2009, each class member was asked to choose a current issue with leadership implications, and to develop a case study scenario and question set. The case studies were required to have a detailed description of the case context, the challenges to be addressed, and concluding questions to be answered that would help students explore key case issues. Students were required to ground their case study in a peer reviewed article. Once created, the case studies were then used throughout the semester, and in subsequent years, to help students to apply and dialogue about leadership and management theories. They were additionally utilized to aid students in applying theory to the context of higher education, and to develop an experiential base upon which to engage in leadership in higher education at multiple organizational levels.

This book of case studies is designed to serve as a resource guide to help higher education students apply higher education leadership and management theories to practice, and to allow them to actively engage in working through diverse institutional issues within assorted institutional contexts. Though this collection of cases was initially created to facilitate the application of theory to practice in small group discussions, individual cases can be easily utilized for more formalized written responses. The cases have been thematically organized within the following broad leadership and management categories: 1) leadership issues; 2) addressing mental health issues; 3) moments of crisis and campus safety; 4) technology in academia; 5) academic freedom; 6) campus diversity; 7) strategic planning and staffing issues; 8) working with student organizations; and 9) policy issues and fiscal tensions. Each case study includes the basic situation that is being presented, the institutional context in which the situation takes place, and tasks and questions for students, or individuals, to discuss.

Table of Contents

Campus Diversity

Strategic Planning and Staffing Issues

Working with Student Organizations

Policy Issues and Fiscal Tensions

Leading and Managing People in Higher Education

Andrew Wall

Basic Situation

You are a member of the student affairs division of a public comprehensive university located in the northeastern United States. Recently, a long-standing and well-loved individual has left vacant the key position of vice-president of student affairs. You and your colleagues have been asked to serve as the search committee to replace the vice-president position. Each member of the search committee represents a different functional area of the university. Your first task is to identify the members of your search committee, and from which areas they hail; there could be members from academic administration, faculty, multiple student affairs departments, and other stakeholders of your groups' choice. You are to report to the president who each person on your team will represent, and also their key list of desires for the new vice-president of student affairs.

Institutional Context

Your institution is a mid-sized public university that grants bachelor's and master's degrees. You have an enrollment of 12,235 with 4,875 students living on campus in the university-owned residence halls. The student population is predominately White. You have about 8,500 undergraduates with the rest being graduate students. In the past decade, the institution has been mostly supported by the state, and as such, the physical structure of the campus is generally in good repair, but not outstanding. Similarly, faculty and administrative salaries are average compared to your peer comprehensive institutions. The average entering SAT score of students at your institution is about 1050. Retention is a major issue, with a six-year graduation rate of only 54 percent, and a one-year retention rate of about 61 percent.

The reputation of the institution is regional, and is seen by students as affordable, but not highly selective. The school is known as being a great "party school," and seems to relish that reputation. The administration is progressively alarmed by student alcohol use and misuse, as there are increasing incidents of students transported to the hospital for alcohol overdose. Another concern on this predominantly White campus is the experience of students of color. The campus has a small, but important, minority population. These students have been vocal in recent years about the lack of sustained institutional support for students of color on campus, and in the rural community in which the institution is located.

The Student Affairs Division Context

The student affairs division was once the crown jewel of the campus. The previous vice- president of student affairs was perceived as progressive, energetic, and transformative, and was able to transmit this enthusiasm to the wider campus community. However, recent years have seen a stagnation of new ideas, and the maintenance of existing programs first developed when the vice-president was new on campus in the early 1990s. Some of these programs include four different-themed living-learning residence halls, a leadership center, a minority student affairs house, and a service-learning program.

The division of student affairs has 241 employees, and, when housing and dining is included, a 41 million dollar annual budget. The division is comprehensive, as it holds the Offices of the Dean of Students, Student Activities, Housing, Admissions, Financial Aid, Recreation, Minority Student Affairs, and Greek Life. Assessment data indicate that compared to peer institutions, student involvement in campus life is average, and faculty consistently speak about the disengagement of students in academic life.

The recent economic downturn in the economy has hit this institution, as it has all institutions. As part of a mid-year budget adjustment, the division of student affairs has recently been asked to give back two percent of its yearly budget; it is likely that next year there will be no increases in the student affairs budget of the incoming vice-president.

Your Task

Your challenge is to complete the following tasks:

1. The admissions committee must organize itself, and then put together a description of the type of candidate that it wants to fill this position;

2. Articulate the traits and behaviors that you think are necessary in a new leader;

3. Put forward a prioritized list of leadership challenges that the incoming leader should identify;

4. Identify a strategy for recruiting the type of leader that you are interested in inviting to this senior leadership role;

5. Please critique your efforts, paying close attention to what leadership values you focused on in both organizing your group, and in arriving at your answers to the responses; and

6. What conceptual grouping(s) of leadership research should you employ in developing your responses and approach?

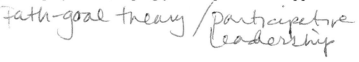

path-goal theory / participative leadership

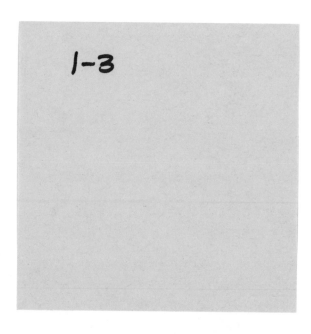

1-3

Your Task

Your challenge is to complete the following tasks:

1. The admissions committee must organize itself, and then put together a description of the type of candidate that it wants to fill this position;

2. Articulate the traits and behaviors that you think are necessary in a new leader;

3. Put forward a prioritized list of leadership challenges that the incoming leader should identify;

4. Identify a strategy for recruiting the type of leader that you are interested in inviting to this senior leadership role;

5. Please critique your efforts, paying close attention to what leadership values you focused on in both organizing your group, and in arriving at your answers to the responses; and

6. What conceptual grouping(s) of leadership research should you employ in developing your responses and approach?

Path-goal theory / participative leadership

School of Acupuncture and Oriental Medicine: Faculty Unrest, a Vote of No Confidence

Michael A. Mestan

Basic Situation

You have been the dean of a school of acupuncture and oriental medicine for about one year. Prior to this position, you were a faculty member at another acupuncture school for seven years. In your position as dean, you oversee a leadership team that is comprised of three faculty members. Each person on the team is assigned leadership responsibilities in areas of the school such as curriculum, clinical education, and research. They are paid a supplementary $3,000 a year for the additional tasks associated with these leadership team positions, and their teaching load is reduced three credit hours per trimester under a normal teaching load. At this time, however, there is a need for them to teach a full load, and so they are paid to teach above what they are contractually required to do. Typically, they are paid an additional $3,000 - 5,000 per year for their course overload.

Over the past few months, you have noticed that the members of the leadership team have been openly disagreeing with you in faculty meetings and around campus. They suggest actions that are good, though very costly, and might limit the number of incoming students. They are constantly working to garner support from the other faculty to agree with them. The situation has deteriorated to the point that you try to avoid them whenever possible, and have resigned to communicate with them through email. The provost just called you in to inform you that your leadership team has met with him. They gave you a vote of no confidence, and are threatening to quit.

Institutional Context

The School of Acupuncture was formed about seven years ago. It was previously run by a dean that hand selected her faculty to include: an ex-president of a larger west coast acupuncture school, his wife, two of their close friends, and two faculty from China who have difficulty speaking English. The husband and wife team are nationally recognized in the acupuncture field, and actively participate in state legislation surrounding the practice of acupuncture. The administration of the college frequently comments on how lucky the school is to have them as faculty. There was a very close relationship between the former dean and the faculty, to the point that friendships were formed outside of work.

The School of Acupuncture is part of a larger natural health education college in a rural setting that has been a chiropractic college for 90 years. The school offers two master's degrees: one in acupuncture (MSA), and one in acupuncture and oriental medicine (MSAOM). Both degrees allow graduates the ability to sit for professional licensure. The program has eight full time faculty members and three adjunct faculty. There are about 65 full-time students who are divided into three cohorts throughout the eight to nine trimester programs. Current enrollment goals for the school are 100 matriculated students with annual increases to reach 150 students.

While the vast majority of the 800 plus students at the college are in the doctor of chiropractic program, the college offers several other master's degrees, including the ones in your school. After a year of poor performance of the financial markets, the endowment has shrunk from 55 million to 35 million. The college has an operating budget of 23 million, and all of its schools are overwhelmingly tuition dependent (85%).

Your Task

Please respond to the following:

1. Describe the situation in terms of informal authority and positional authority;

2. Describe the situation in terms of group and team dynamics, and what type of group leadership skills (action) are needed by you, the dean. By the provost?

3. What actions or steps should the dean take given the context of his limited power and influence?

4. Describe what relationship should exist between the dean and provost utilizing the power and influence theory.

Addressing Mental Health Issues at a Private Institution

Michelle Rogers

Basic Situation

You are the president of a private institution located in the Northeast. You have been in your role for three years, and have been successful at implementing some broad changes that have been received well by the faculty, staff, students, and community. You have a strong team of senior leaders with whom you meet weekly, all with varying personalities and skill sets. Precipitated by a recent student suicide (the second in the academic year), you have asked each of your senior leaders to provide you with a three-page report examining the mental health issues facing the students within his/her respective schools, and outlining how the school is currently addressing them.

Institutional Context

Founded in 1890 by wealthy businessmen, and in collaboration with a Baptist society, the main campus is nestled on the outskirts of a metropolitan area, with a few buildings located within the city itself. The first university president envisioned a new and modern research university that combined an English-style undergraduate college, and a German-style graduate research institute. Currently, the university enrolls 4,900 undergraduate students, and 10,220 graduate, professional, and other students. It is supported by 2,175 faculty and other academic personnel. You have 142,360 alumni worldwide. The undergraduate college offers 52 majors, and 24 minors, spanning the humanities, physical sciences, social sciences, and biological sciences. Undergraduate tuition is $36,175. There are six graduate professional schools: a Divinity School, a School of Business, a Law School, a School of Medicine, a School of Public Policy Studies, and a School of Social Service Administration. Your institution also offers degree, certificate, and open enrollment programs through a School of General Studies.

Your school is a member of the Association of American Universities (AAU), and is a national leader in higher education and research; it is known as an institution unafraid to try new things and face difficult challenges. Last year, your institution sponsored research awards that totaled $428.5 million. The university has filed more than 3,600 patents since 1985.

Your campus is closely connected with the diverse community, and involved in many partnerships that help to serve the institution and to support the community. You employ 15,000 people (including the medical center). This year, the university's consolidated operating revenue was $2.9 billion, and the endowment value was $4.2 billion.

The College Context and the Current Mental Health Services

The college boasts a diverse student population from a variety of socioeconomic backgrounds. Students hail from a multiplicity of geographic locations, with the largest percentage coming from the Midwest and Mid-Atlantic, followed by the West Coast, New England, the South, and the Southwest. The current class includes 1,260 students: 49 percent men, and 51 percent women, including 81 African-American students, 98 Latino students, and 123 international students.

The college has a student counseling and resource center that provides various services, primarily to undergraduates. This care includes mental health assessments, emergency services, crisis intervention, therapy (individual, couples, and group), medication management, academic skills counseling, and referral services. Additionally, the center provides consultation to university officials, faculty, and staff who have concerns about a student. While there are several programs and services provided, many students do not take advantage of them, and there is little outreach to, or support for, graduate students. The programs have not been evaluated or modified in over five years. Resident assistants receive little to no training in this area, but have been asking for support for the past two years. There have been a few attempts to launch education and awareness programs, but they have failed due to lack of support and participation. There has been some success with reaching freshman during orientation, but more can be done. There is also a group of engaged medical students who have been trying to get some outreach programs started.

Your Task

First, you need to review the reports you have asked your senior leaders to prepare, and work with them to evaluate the effectiveness of the mental health services currently provided. Second, you need to determine if changes need to be made to address the increase in the severity and number of mental health problems among your student population. You believe that changes are needed to handle the increase in the number of students needing and/or seeking mental health services, and to provide proactive support more effectively.

In your effort to implement changes, consider the following questions as you review the current state of mental health support on your campus:

1. How do you feel about your institution's current mental health programs? What do your senior leaders believe needs to be done, if anything? What approaches to leadership will you use?

2. Who will you involve in the process, and what leadership techniques will you use to do so? What role, if any, will the students have in making decisions/suggestions in the case scenario? Parents? Community?

3. What are the major leadership responsibilities in this case study? Faculty responsibilities? Student responsibilities? Parent responsibilities?

4. In light of current budget restraints due to the global economic crisis, how will you fund suggested changes? What leadership methods will you use to get funding?

5. Articulate the process by which you will implement proposed changes to your institution's mental health services. In doing so, outline your leadership plan.

Addressing Crisis at an Urban Community College

Andrew Wall

Basic Situation

You and your team are all administrators and faculty at an urban community college in upstate New York. The community college is located in an eight story building in the downtown area of a major city of two million people. The community college occupies four different floors of the building, with other floors being occupied by businesses of various types. Just after noon today, there was a multi-car accident in which a car was sent through the front doors of the building that houses the college. The car entered the front of the building, traveled 25 feet, and crashed into the bank of elevators that assist individuals in accessing the college which is located at least three floors above ground level. The car that entered the front of the building was driven by a student of the college. Ten people were injured from shattered glass, and the car's impact. Of the ten injured individuals from inside the building, four of them are students of the college who were awaiting an elevator.

Institutional Context

The urban community college is a branch campus of a larger community college institution. The urban college serves 1,800 students in FTE, but there are over 3,900 students enrolled part- or full-time during this year's spring semester at the college. The students at the college are predominantly minority in ethnicity, with 62 percent of the students of African descent, 28 percent are Latino/a, and 10 percent of other ethnic backgrounds. Students at the college tend to be first generation college students, with a large population being adult students who also hold full-time jobs somewhere in the city. Due to the small number of students, and the central housing of the campus in one building, the sense of community at the campus is very strong. The college boasts solid programs in human services, criminal justice, liberal arts, and college preparation.

The Crisis Team Context

You and your team are part of the small group of full-time administrators on campus, along with one of you being a faculty member/student advisor. Your team is responsible for academic administration (i.e. scheduling courses, grades, etc.), registration, advising, student services, and campus life. Your campus does have a crisis team, of which the members of your group are all members (i.e. your group is the crisis team). The crisis team is responsible for both policy and campus response to the crisis situation.

Your Task

Your task for this case study is to address the following issues:

1. What are the immediate needs from the perspective of your crisis response team? What actions will you take over the next 24, 48 and 72 hours?

2. What is unique about the community college context of this situation?

3. Is this a crisis? Or is this some other type of event?

4. What are the major leadership responsibilities of this situation? What are the management responsibilities?

5. Is there an identified process that you will follow in this situation (i.e. a crisis response plan)?

6. What type of leadership approach or theory will you use to guide your actions in response to this situation?

Update One

You have just been informed that one of those injured in the accident has died of his/her injuries. The individual who passed away was a student at the college for the past three semesters, and was highly involved in student life.

1. Does this change your response plan?

2. How will you respond to this new development?

3. What is needed now from leadership, which may or may not have been needed before?

Update Two

You have just learned from the police that the cause of the accident was drug or alcohol related. The involved student driver is known on campus to have an alcohol use problem, and was headed home after having attended class.

1. How does this impact your response to the situation in the short and long term?

2. How does this new information influence the role the leadership might play in this situation?

Leadership Challenges in Crisis and in a Bureaucracy

Rudy Greg Trejo

Basic Situation

You are the newly appointed president of a small, private university located in the southwest region of the United States. Recently, your school has received several bomb threats, most occurring in the residence halls. All of the threats have proved to be empty, often resulting in no arrests or further action being needed. With every threat, all buildings are vacated, campus is locked down, classes are postponed, and local police are brought out onto campus. A net loss of nearly $10,000 occurs during each threat. Last week, a bomb threat was once again made, this time, directed toward a residence hall on campus. The director of Residence Life has stated that because this is a frequent occurrence that has resulted in no discoveries, no evacuation is needed. Aside from a brief search of the building by the University Police Department no further action should be taken, and classes should go on as scheduled. The vice-president for Student Affairs, the direct supervisor of the director of Residence Life, agrees with the director.

You agree with both the director and vice president to essentially ignore the threat and conduct business as usual. Hours later, a small explosion is heard in the distance. It is reported to you that a small fire bomb was set off in the residence hall where the note stated the event would occur. While no injuries or damage to the residence hall occurred, the event has left you shaken. In the school's newspaper released the week following the incident, it was reported that both the director of Residence Life and vice-president for Student Affairs were aware of the note, and failed to act. A petition has spread calling for both of their resignations.

Institutional Context

Your institution is Roman Catholic affiliated, with strong ties to its faith, history, and mission. Historically, the institution was founded in 1885 by a Catholic priest, with the idea of allowing farmers to continue with their education. The institution now enrolls 5,300 students, with 3,500 full time undergraduates, and the remainder graduate students. The college includes five schools and offers bachelor's and master's degrees. The institution houses nearly 1,300 undergraduate students in its six residence halls and one apartment complex. The institution has grown by nearly 1,000 students during your predecessor's ten year tenure as president. The endowment also doubled to $5.8 million, as did awards and recognition, including significant strides in the *U.S. News and World Reports* rankings. Your predecessor was loved by the students, and admired by faculty and staff, and, as a result, was given the title *President Emeritus* by the Board of Trustees. In addition, the vice-president of Student Affairs and director of Residence Life also played significant roles in the growth of the institution, and have gained respect and admiration amongst the college community.

College President Context

You have only been at the college for one month when the bomb incident occurs. Given the "large shoes" you must fill from the popularity of your predecessor, you are facing issues of lack of respect from students, faculty, and staff. Additionally, due to the long tenure and respect for the vice-president of Student Affairs, and the director of Residence Life, people on campus are seeking leadership guidance from them, rather than from you.

Your Task

The school paper has asked for an interview with you to get a better sense of what occurred. In speaking with the vice-president of Student Affairs and director of Residence Life, you have told them of the interview request. Both individuals see this as an opportunity for you, as president, to place a firm foot, and to gain the respect of the college. They have both given you the "okay" to place sole blame of the incident on them, granted that you guarantee both of their jobs. However, your general counsel has warned that keeping both individuals opens up the college to lawsuits. The local city newspapers have also heard about the incident, and will gain several of their facts from the interview you will give to the campus newspaper. Your responses will set the tone for the next step of your presidency. The newspaper has sent questions ahead of time. Your task is to decide how you will respond to them. In your answers, think about the historical context of your institution, as well as your current position. Can you do more as a leader by denying the blame, or, do you step up and acknowledge your role in the decision not to evacuate the residence halls? If you choose to acknowledge your role, what will be your argument? If you choose to place the responsibility on your vice-president and director, what happens to them and the incident? Be sure to use leadership theory in guiding your responses. How much does leadership play in this situation?

Your task is to consider the student newspaper questions below, and to then respond to the questions that follow:

1. After the note was discovered, when was a decision made to not evacuate the residence hall?

2. Were you, as university president, informed of the threat? If so, when?

3. Who made the decision to continue classes and not evacuate the hall?

4. Were you involved in the decision? If so, how much of the decision was yours?

5. Given that an actual bomb was found, what will happen to the vice-president of Student Affairs and the director of Residence Life?

6. As president, how much of the responsibility do you take?

7. What plans will the university take to address the situation? Will a committee be formed? To what extent will the local police be involved?

Questions for Discussion

Given the situation you now find yourself in as president, please respond to the following:

8. What are the ethical questions presented in this situation?

9. In this situation, what responsibilities does the president have?

10. What steps should the leader in this situation take immediately, as well as over the next weeks and months?

11. How real is this situation? What makes it either "real" or exaggerated?

12. What theories of leadership can give practical action in this case?

Robbery on Campus

Michael Edelman

Basic Situation

You represent the administration of a large, private university in a suburban area that is only a ten minute drive from a 100,000 person city. The college is located on a 1,000-plus acre campus, and has multiple residence halls, dining facilities, and college buildings. You were notified at 7am that there was a robbery at 6:30am this morning in a new dining facility located on the outskirts of the campus buildings. Three workers were opening up for breakfast at the time of the robbery. Two men in masks rushed through the unlocked back door and demanded money from the safe. As the suspects fled through the back door, one of them shot at two of the workers. Both of the workers suffered mild gunshot wounds (one worker was shot in the lower right leg, and the other had a bullet graze her arm), but no one was critically injured. The third worker was in a separate area at the time of the robbery and placed the 911 call.

Institutional Context

The university serves almost 14,000 undergraduate students and about 2,700 graduate students. The undergraduate college has a reputation as a party school, but has had minimal incidents of violent crimes. There are over 70 small and large buildings on campus, including the residence halls, and over 70 emergency "blue light" phones that call directly to university security and EMT services. The university is also notorious for having a low retention rate that it has been battling to raise, and has recently identified the issue as a top priority.

Approximately 6,800 students live on campus full time, and eat all of their meals at the dining halls. Almost 5,000 nonresident students have a partial meal plan. Due to its large campus and farmland bordering the southern part of the college, the school is able to boast about its rural feel in a suburban area. The campus is a ten minute drive from a medium sized city with a rich cultural history, but that also has a reputation for consistently being in the top ten for crime in mid-sized cities. The university is well known for its engineering, computer science, liberal arts, nursing, and business programs.

Your Task

Even though you are at a large, private university, you do not have a crisis team or a general crisis plan. Nonetheless, you do have a large public relations and marketing department at your disposal. Please respond to the following questions:

1. How will you immediately address the crisis with the university's community (students, parents, faculty and staff, and the local community surrounding the campus), and what modes of communication will you use?

    a. Who will be your main spokesperson?

    b. Who is the lead manager of your crisis team, and what other administrators/faculty complete your team?

    c. What leadership behaviors or theories will leadership and management utilize to manage this crisis?

2. Are certain leadership approaches more effective at communicating information across different forms of media?

    a. If so, how will you change your leadership approach when releasing the same information through different forms of media?

3. A short term crisis plan for the next one to four weeks should be developed to meet the needs of this specific situation, and to ensure students and parents that the university is safe.

    a. What does the plan entail, and how will the plan be communicated to the university community?

4. How will you address this incident with prospective students, and the people who influence their decisions on where to attend college?

    a. Why is it especially important to target this group?

Reacting to a Public Health Crisis

Joseph Parker

Institutional Context

Brook College is a private institution in upstate New York located approximately 100 miles from a major metropolitan area. The college primarily serves undergraduate students, but has grown its graduate program over the last two years since the new president came on board. Presently, the college has an undergraduate population of 6,448, and a graduate student population of 1,417. The college seeks a diverse population of students, in particular international students. Twelve percent of the student body, both undergraduate and graduate, is made up of international students. The international students represent 79 different nations. Domestically, the college primarily draws from the east coast states.

Basic Situation

The college is presently on winter recess, but the spring semester will be starting in another week. Most students have left the school for home or elsewhere, however a large percentage of the international students stay on campus during the break. Along with the international students, there are students attending a college workshop, and others who stay due to work obligations. This is a quiet time for the college, and both faculty and staff often use the break to travel for vacation. The exception is the Enrollment Office, which has been busy running campus tours for perspective students.

Despite being a quiet time, the Health Center has seen an increase of students with flu-like symptoms. During the winter recess, the Health Center lowers staffing levels from those scheduled during when classes are in session. The Health Center is presently running on a skeleton crew. The higher than normal volume of drop-in students with flu-like symptoms is starting to overwhelm the staff.

On Saturday, a student treated by the Health Center the previous week was taken to the hospital by ambulance. A roommate concerned about his condition called campus security, which resulted in the ambulance being called. On Sunday, the local news reports on the student, as well as the regional increase in flu-like symptoms, and incidents of other non-student hospitalizations. On Monday, the national press picks up the story, and runs stories on the student (who remains hospitalized), the regional incidences, pandemics, and a related story on a population in New Jersey that is also seeing an unusually high incident of flu-like symptoms with hospitalizations. Meanwhile, the Heath Center continues to see a high volume of students with similar symptoms, and continues to advise rest and over the counter medications. Campus security has received an increase in calls from parents who are concerned because they have not been able to reach their on-campus son or daughter. By Tuesday, a significant portion of the on-campus student population, as well as a number of staff members, most notably in the Enrollment Office, are ill. There have been additional hospitalizations. It is clear that there is a health problem. The college is being contacted by concerned students and parents. The press is now on campus daily. Classes start in six days.

Challenges

The president has faced leadership challenges in the past two years, but this is her first with intense public scrutiny. The college relies on the Health Center to address typical student health concerns, but it is not equipped or positioned to handle a major health crisis. Being in a rural location, the available public health services support a large geographic area with limited resources. Campus security has limited communications with the Health Center, and they do not report incidences which require outside medical attention back to the Health Center. The college is working on an emergency notification system, but only limited testing has been completed. Currently, the only means of communicating directly with undergraduates is through email. The central student information system is obsolete and lacks student information, such as students' cell phone numbers, or out of school contact information. There is emergency contact information in the student information system, but it is not updated after a student first matriculates.

Your Task

The college needs to respond to this crisis. You are one of a number of senior administrative staff that has been assembled midday to construct a response plan to deal with the safety of the students, faculty, and staff. You and the team must construct a response and communication plan by tomorrow morning for the president, with the expectation of immediate execution. Your plan must include a recommendation about whether the start of classes should be delayed.

Update One

The student who was hospitalized is the son of alumni who met at Brook College. The couple has successful careers, and are generous contributors to the College. Through communication with their son's roommate, they have just discovered that he is in the hospital. They are furious that the college did not notify them. Before the team meets with the president, the parents have contacted the president's office to express their dissatisfaction. When reviewing the plan, the team is now directed to additionally respond on a personal level for any hospitalized students. The president's first concern is for the safety of the students, faculty and staff, but the team knows that the way in which this situation is handled will reflect on the president, and will affect her ability to draw interest in giving financial support to the college. How will the team address both the broad plan and the personal issues?

1. What are the major issues present in this case example?
2. What individuals within the university should be a part of the response to this health crisis?
3. What approach to leadership should be adopted by the senior administrative staff? What would be the most ideal approach, and what would be the most likely response?

Safety Concerns for Students Abroad

Chelsea BaileyShea

Basic Situation

You are the dean of students. You have held this position for the past twelve years, but have worked at your institution for over twenty years. You began your career in the Modern Languages Department as a French professor. In your capacity as a French professor, you were dedicated to increasing the awareness of study abroad opportunities to students on campus. Though you felt that it was critical for foreign language majors to study abroad, you felt equally strongly that this was an experience from which all undergraduates would benefit. When you began working at your school over twenty years ago, only 13 percent of students studied abroad. Today, the number has risen to 30 percent. Your goal has always been to make it 100 percent. After years of discussion about this goal with the president, and countless meetings with other faculty and administrators, you were finally able to put a study abroad graduation requirement forward to the Faculty Senate. Though there were a number of faculty members opposed to this idea—citing the lack of academic rigor in many study abroad programs, as well as financial complications for certain students (a potential drawback with regard to admissions recruitment)—the new graduation requirement passed.

You are committed to the value of students studying abroad, and fought tirelessly to accomplish this goal. To address the financial concern, you successfully argued for the transference of financial aid. Moreover, to defray some of the travel expenses, your college will offer a one-time voucher of between $1,200 to $3,000, to each student enrolled full-time in a degree-seeking program. The amount of the voucher will depend upon the length of time the student studies abroad (e.g. summer, semester, full-year). You view student global mindedness as an essential personal skill (and second language acquisition, if possible), but when speaking with high level administrators, you often frame this new initiative as a positive marketing opportunity for your school, as you are the first American college to require this of its graduating students.

This is the first year in which all newly matriculated students are required to study abroad before graduation. It is mid-November, and the Office of Study Abroad is in full swing with spring and summer study abroad applications. Students studying overseas during the fall semester are already well into the semester in their host countries. While attending a student affairs conference, the director of the Office of Study Abroad calls to tell you that last night there was a bombing in a Parisian nightclub that is known to be popular with Americans abroad. Thirty people were taken to the hospital to be treated for serious to mild injuries, and there are nine known fatalities, six of them American undergraduates abroad. Though none of the six dead American students is from your own college, there were at least two students from your institution who were at the nightclub that night. Thankfully, both had left the club before the bombing took place a little after midnight. You prepare to leave the conference, knowing that you will need to address this situation with administrators at your school, as well as concerned parents and students.

Institutional Context

Your institution is a small, private, highly selective liberal arts school located on the East Coast. You have an undergraduate enrollment of 3,200 students, and a small number of M.A/M.S graduate students (100). You only accept 14 percent of all applicants who apply. Although the comprehensive fee for room, board, and tuition at your school is high ($52,150), at least 50 percent of students receive some form of financial aid, either in the form of federal grants or scholarships. The majority of your undergraduate students are of traditional age (18-22), and all but a very small minority, mostly "return to college" students, live full-time in a variety of residence options on campus. Each year, your admissions team strives to create a diverse class, and you pride yourself on the high number of international students who attend your college (19%). Ethnically, your student population is predominately White/Caucasian (55%), with the remaining population being 20 percent Asian, 10 percent Latino, eight percent African-American, three percent Native-American, and the remaining four percent not self-identifying. Students are represented by all of the 50 states, and come from more than 75 different countries.

Your Task

Your challenge is to create a policy response for how you will address the concerns of the key stakeholders: students, parents, and administrators.

Initial Questions:

1. Who will you consult as you construct your policy regarding current and future students abroad?

2. Once you have a policy in place, what will you say to concerned parents who call your office?

Update One

A terrorist organization has claimed responsibility for this attack. They are angry with the European and American stance on the war in the Middle East, and they have released a video in which they state that this is only the beginning of their assault. The European Union and American government have issued travel warnings. Both your and the provost's offices are being inundated with calls from the concerned parents of current students abroad, in Europe, in particular. Many other parents of students who will be studying abroad in the spring are saying they no longer know if they support their children studying overseas. Additionally, some faculty and staff are now questioning the new study abroad graduation requirement. There are a number who are openly wondering if it might result in a less competitive applicant pool, as more and more parents worry about their child's safety. You are worried that all of your hard work in putting study abroad at the forefront of the curriculum might soon disappear.

Question:

1. What is your plan of action as you deal with faculty, administrators, and parents who are now opposed to the study abroad graduation requirement?

Update Two

There are currently 20 students from your college studying in Paris. The director of the Paris program calls to tell you that half of them want to come home. Additionally, you have received calls from parents of students studying in other locations saying they wanted their child to return home. There are only four weeks left in the semester at your school, making this an awkward time for these students to return to campus in terms of credits/enrollment.

Additional Questions

1. What will your policy be for students wishing to return home?

2. How will your policy affect advising for students planning to study abroad in the spring? Will you discourage them from certain locations?

3. What approach to leadership will guide your actions?

4. Please identify key issues to be addressed in the case, and what you will consider in making your decisions.

5. Who will you consult in making choices in terms of how to address the challenges of the case?

Social Media and its Impact on an Institution

Kristen Emery

Basic Situation

You are the provost at a mid-sized, private university located in the mid-western United States. You have been in your current position for the past eight years, and were previously a tenured faculty member at the university prior to your appointment as provost. You pride yourself on being an involved, student-centered provost, whose door is always open. You aim for an interconnected dialogue-centered learning and administrative environment at the university. After fielding questions and listening to recent complaints from faculty about students who routinely post status updates to Facebook and other social media websites during class lectures, you being to consider the negative ramifications of socially-accepted around-the-clock social media connections and website-use on campus.

You consider the many connection and ease-of use benefits of websites such as Facebook, but then research the topic on your own only to learn the shockingly high number of minutes that college students typically spend on Facebook each week (147 minutes). You also discover that it has become a social norm across many college campuses, including your own, for students to log into Facebook to post status updates and send messages to others while in class.

Some of the faculty have recently voiced to you that they have even witnessed students commenting and complaining about their lectures in real-time on Facebook. Along with the faculty, you are particularly concerned about students logging onto Facebook and other social media websites while in class. Furthermore, on a series on walks around campus in the last two weeks, you observe that while hallways and outdoor gathering spots on campus used to buzz with student conversations, now the buzz seems to be coming primarily from cell-phone rings and laptop sounds chiming with messages for students logged into Facebook and other websites.

Institutional Context

Your institution is a mid-sized, private university in the Midwest that grants bachelor's and master's degrees. You have an enrollment of 9,617, with about 7,090 undergraduate students, and the rest graduate students. Eighty-one percent of new freshmen live on-campus, and approximately 5,700 undergraduates live on campus in total. You have a large amount of undergraduates who live on-campus largely because of the newly completed apartment-style dorms that the university finished building and furnishing the previous summer. Sixty-two percent of students are full-time students. There are 426 faculty in total, and the student/faculty ratio is 16:1. The university puts a great amount of faith in their faculty and administrative leaders, and aims to provide a forward thinking, innovative learning environment. This is reflected in the university's 2001 decision to include a laptop and service coverage as part of the cost of tuition for all full-time undergraduates and graduate students. Your predecessor implemented this program one year before you became provost. You have continued to support the program for a variety of reasons, but primarily because it saves students and the university money regarding computer service, hardware, and software needs.

Your Task

You have decided that you would like to gain the support of key administrative leaders in order to implement a weeklong, campus-wide ban on Facebook, MySpace, and Twitter. The ban would affect the wireless internet and campus internet sources that the university houses, including all university-owned dorms and apartments. Internet-capable cell-phones and private internet connections could not and would not be affected. Your reasons for the ban are centered around the notion that you wish to encourage faculty, staff, and students to become more aware of the following: 1) their reliance on social media websites; 2) how often they feel the need to post to a social media website, as opposed to speaking to someone in person; 3) what they use social media for; 4) the text and images that they post; and finally 5) the people (whom they may or may not know) who are able to obtain access to view the posted text and images. You also hope to encourage more direct social interaction, and perhaps stimulate future interest in more face-to-face interactions. As you move to address the following issues, you must determine how you will organize this initiative and its challenges. Your initial tasks are the following:

1. Describe how you will move forward to consider the idea of implementing your plan for a weeklong, campus-wide ban on Facebook, MySpace, and Twitter. Who will you approach first, and in what format? Whose input/permission will you seek first and why?

2. What type of leadership approach or theory will you use to guide your actions and presentation of this idea to fellow administrative leaders, faculty, and staff? What leadership traits and behaviors will you utilize to garner support from institutional members?

3. Assuming you successfully gain support for this initiative, how will you inform faculty, staff, and students that the ban will occur and when it will begin and end?

4. What are the risk factors to consider in implementing this ban? How will you manage students who respond to the ban by utilizing social media websites on their cell-phones and off-campus? How do issues of power and influence play into the implementation and the carrying out of the weeklong ban?

5. What is your long-term strategy for when the ban is lifted? How will you encourage faculty and students to view the weeklong ban, and reflect on their perceived reliance on social media as opposed to face-to-face conversations?

6. How will you assess the success of the ban? Will you urge faculty and staff to adjust their social media online habits while on campus? What type of leadership will work best as you address this issue for/with faculty and staff?

Update One

Five days into the now approved and implemented weeklong, campus-wide ban on Facebook, MySpace, and Twitter.

The campus-wide ban is going as well as could be expected. There are students who use their cell phones to gain access to social media websites, and some who head to off-campus coffee shops to get around the ban. Overall, you notice that the ban introduced an obstacle to social media reliance, and students do appear to be engaging in more face-to-face interaction in classes and around campus.

However, on Friday morning you receive an email from an undergraduate student. The email contains a Facebook status update that appears to have been posted by a new male junior faculty member whom you know. It appears that this undergraduate student logged into Facebook (perhaps via a cell phone or off-campus) and read a status update that his English professor had posted to Facebook earlier this morning. It is unclear how this student obtained access to the professor's Facebook page, or whether or not the student and the professor are Facebook "friends," which the administration actively discourages. The student has copied and pasted this status update into an email, and has now sent it to you. In his Facebook status update, the faculty member appeared to have posted "Wow, for once my students are actually paying attention ---that's never happened. Long live the Facebook ban!" As you read this email, you consider the many issues regarding what this undergraduate student has now forwarded to you.

1. How do power and influence play into this complex situation? How will you assess the validity of this email, and the faculty member's apparent Facebook status update, which may have been posted on campus (perhaps via a cell phone) while the ban is still in effect?

2. To whom will you respond regarding this recent email (the student, the faculty member, etc.) and whom will you inform of this email?

3. Will this email change the fact that the ban is scheduled to last another two days? Given your earlier observations of increased communication interactions and engaged reflection on social media reliance on campus, will this email change the way you currently view the success of the ban?

Making Changes in Higher Education

Andrew Wall

Basic Situation

You are a faculty member of a public comprehensive university located in the northeastern United States. You are an early adopter of technology in the classroom, and are very interested in developing on-line learning opportunities for students. You and your colleagues have been asked to lead an effort to create an on-line master's degree program in higher education administration. Each member of the committee represents a different stakeholder in the process. Your first task is to identify what area each of your committee members are from: there could be members from academic administration, faculty, students, and other stakeholders of your group's choice. You are to report to the department chair the areas included in your team, and which role each person on your team will play. You will also provide recommendations as to if, how, and what, should be done about creating an on-line master's degree in higher education administration.

Institutional Context

Your institution is a private research university that grants bachelor's, master's, Ed.D. and Ph.D. degrees. You have an enrollment of 14,353 with 4,875 students living on campus in the university-owned residence halls. You have about 10,500 undergraduates with the rest being graduate students. The College of Human Ecology and Education has about 1,560 students, of whom 950 are undergraduates majoring in some form of teacher preparation. The higher education graduate program has 84 currently enrolled students, with 54 being Ed.D. and Ph.D., and 30 being master's degree students. The program has 3.5 FTE faculty, plus a cadre of regular adjunct instructors.

The reputation of the program is regional, and is seen as rigorous, but small. The program has a strong group of doctoral graduates working in higher education administration and faculty positions. There are fewer identified master's graduates working broadly in the region. The faculty from the program includes one tenured, and two junior tenure track faculty, along with a .5 appointment of another tenured faculty member that holds a joint appointment. The program has not changed in faculty size in a number of years, but the enrollment of students has decreased from a high of 115 to the current level.

The Challenge of On-Line

The 12 faculty members in the educational leadership department in which the master's degree program is housed are not a technology proficient group, and have abhorred the notion of on-line courses. Rather, the faculty would like to keep classes on-campus, and small. Feedback from the students is that the program has been decreasing in size due to the outdated curriculum, and the lack of student centeredness of the program, and from the faculty.

Your Task

At your own initiative, you are spearheading an effort to create a planning committee and "explore" the idea of offering a degree program on-line. Your challenge is to:

1. Create a plan for how you will organize yourself;

2. Articulate how you plan to move forward to consider the idea of implementing an on-line degree program, one that would be the first for the school; and

3. Identify your leadership approach or style that you will use in exploring this idea.

Update One

During the faculty meeting, one faculty member voices strong opposition to your efforts, even though you have just begun, saying, "We will never have an on-line program as long as I am here." On the other hand, the department chair likes your idea, but wants a financial breakdown and argument before moving forward to the dean.

1. How do you respond to this dynamic? Please attend to your leadership and management thinking.

Academic Freedom:
Religious Studies and Indoctrination

Nahoko Kawakyu-O'Connor

Basic Situation

You are the department chair of the religious studies department at a large, public university in the Midwest. Recently, you received an anonymous letter from a student in the class "American Catholic History," taught by one of the adjunct professors, complaining that the professor has repeatedly said inflammatory and insensitive things, particularly to those who did not share the Catholic religion. The student continued to say that the professor did not allow for any dissent or discussion that went against the Catholic teachings, and has repeatedly claimed that homosexuality was against the natural laws of man. You set up a private meeting with the adjunct professor, during which he denies the claims made in the letter by the student, and states that the lectures and discussions in the classroom reflect the contractual content. He remains adamant that his discussions surrounding the Catholic Church were not indoctrinating in nature. He goes on to say that the student must have misinterpreted the context and concept of the stance on homosexuality in the Catholic Church as stemming from his own opinion, rather than an explanation of the church's position. You believe his account is satisfactory, remind him of his contractual agreement, and the meeting comes to an end. Because the letter was sent anonymously, no specific response was made to the complaint letter.

Three weeks later, you receive another complaint letter, expressing similar concerns regarding the same adjunct professor. This time, the letter is signed with a student's name, as well as an attached copy of the complaint submitted to the editor of the student newsletter, the college president, and the Faculty Senate.

Institutional Context

The institution at which you work is the state's flagship public university situated in the Midwest. Your school has an annual enrollment of 13,000 undergraduate students, and 8,000 graduate students. Students hail from all 50 states, but the majority of the students are from within, and around, the surrounding states. Together, the Asian-American, African-American, Latino, and Native American students comprise less than 10 percent of the student body. The university consists of a School of Letters and Sciences, a Health Professional School, and several other professional schools, including the School of Education, Law School, Business School, and the School of Engineering. The institution is committed to its research faculty, and like most universities, the majority of federal and other outside research funding is brought in by the faculty who reside within the natural sciences and engineering schools.

Departmental Context

The religion department, along with several other humanities and social science departments, has been severely affected by the shift in funding resources for grants and research funds. Recently, they have had to replace several full-time faculty positions with considerably more cost effective part-time adjunct faculty. The adjunct faculty have specifically been given instruction that the teachings in the class must be relevant to the subject for which they were hired to teach, and that 'indoctrination' was prohibited in the classroom. Your department consists of 17 full time professors, and has about seven to eight adjunct professors who are appointed on a yearly basis. Unaware of the recent letters of complaint, one of the tenured faculty approaches you and informs you that there is a departmental rumor that a student complained about indoctrination by one of the adjunct professors. This professor, known for her politically liberal leanings, is recognized to have had heated discussions with the adjunct professor during departmental meetings. To your surprise, however, she adamantly defends the adjunct professor's academic freedom, and his right to present controversial materials in the classroom.

Your Task

Your main task is to determine how to proceed in order to find out whether the adjunct professor has violated the faculty code of conduct, and the contractual agreement.

1. As the chair of the department, what would be your first response to the second letter?

2. How will you respond to the tenured faculty member?

3. How will you respond to the student who sent the letter?

4. While the campus editor was copied on the email, the letter has not yet been published in the newspaper. Will you contact the campus editor?

5. Would you handle the case differently if the accused were a tenured professor?

6. What kind of varying leadership challenges may be present as the head of an academic department, as opposed to being in a leadership position in an administrative department?

Addressing Diversity Issues in Higher Education

Andrew Wall

Basic Situation

Your university leadership has recently begun to revitalize efforts to address issues of diversity on campus. The institution has created a new diversity statement that specifically notes institutional support for individuals of different genders, racial/ethnic backgrounds, abilities, sexual orientation and social history. A Provost Office position has been created to coordinate and address issues of diversity on campus. The new diversity officer, housed in the Provost Office, has formed a campus diversity committee to bring forward multiple organizational viewpoints on campus climate, institutional policy, and campus practices associated with issues of diversity on campus.

Initial work on the campus diversity committee has revealed areas of real concern for the institution, including dynamics such as:

1. Recruitment and retention of faculty of color. Statistics reveal the recruitment and retention of faculty of color lags behind faculty from majority groups and comparison institutions;

2. Recent high profile cases of departure of tenured faculty who are women and faculty of color;

3. A lower percentage of successfully tenured women and faculty of color than at comparison institutions;

4. Statistics that indicate the institution fails to attract and matriculate students of color in increasing numbers; and

5. Data suggesting that the graduation rate for students of color, of all backgrounds, is lower than majority (White) students.

Upon receipt of a report of these findings, the provost and the president have recently announced three institutional initiatives to promote a campus commitment to diversity. First, the president announced the creation of a new position that will work jointly between the Admissions Office, the Financial Aid Office, and the Office of Minority Student Affairs, to coordinate a holistic approach to minority student recruitment, retention and success. Second, the provost announced a new fund to support minority faculty recruitment and retention. Third, the provost announced the formation of a pilot mentoring program for all junior faculty, but with specific attention to issues faced by women and minority junior faculty in the early career stage of faculty life.

Institutional Context

Your institution is a private research university located in the northeastern United States. It has an excellent academic reputation, and a long history of outstanding research. The institution's endowment exceeds four billion dollars. It has an enrollment of 14,353 students, of which 4,875 students live on campus in the university-owned residence halls. You have about 10,500 undergraduates with the remainder being graduate students. You work for the School of Education, where there are 1,241 students enrolled in bachelor's and graduate degree granting programs.

Your School and Department Context

The school of education in which you work is one of the most diverse on campus. There are more women than men, along with 24 percent of the faculty being individuals of diverse racial and ethnic backgrounds. The school prides itself on being a place that values diversity, diverse learners, and creating a safe space for students. While this ethos is commonly held, the school recently conducted its environmental study of faculty and staff perceptions of the school culture, and found areas of real concern. First, some faculty of color report feeling as though they are a token minority, and that their diverse background is appreciated for its symbolic nature, rather than its substantive diverse perspective. Second, there have been departures over the last few years by women and faculty of color. Taken as distinct events, these departures can be viewed as individual decisions by faculty to accept new professional opportunities. However, when considered collectively, they may represent a concerning departure trend of capable faculty of diverse backgrounds.

Your department is a particularly diverse department, with more women than men, and 50 percent of the faculty come from minority backgrounds. The department has been successful in recruiting new capable diverse faculty, but is concerned about ensuring the success and retention of new faculty. The students in your departmental programs are also particularly diverse; thirty-five percent report being from racial or ethnic minority backgrounds, and a number of students being openly gay or lesbian in their sexual orientation.

The Incident

Recently, following a class discussion about diversity, you overhear racially bigoted comments from three students in a discussion that occurred as the students were walking out of the class.

Your Task

Your task is to respond to the following questions regarding both the incident you overheard as a student, and the steps the administration has made surrounding the diversity issues at the school:

1. What should you do as a student in response to the racist comments you overheard after class? How does your behavior relate to ideas of leadership?

2. What do you think of the response to issues of diversity by the institution thus far?

3. Has the institution begun to show leadership related to issues of diversity on campus?

4. What do you think of the context of this school of education and department in relationship to their organizational climate related to diversity?

5. Are there any leadership steps to be taken in relation to what you have read thus far?

Update One

You were not the only student who overheard the bigoted discussion. Two other classmates overheard the discussion and have gone to the course instructor to express their concerns. They state that the comments make them feel as though this classroom is an unsafe learning environment for them. The instructor decides to discuss the incident with the class at the next class meeting. She articulates that racial bigoted comments are not acceptable in the context of their class, or as a future and present educator. The faculty member facilitates a classroom discussion in which significant tensions surrounding issues of diversity surface. Collectively, the students are very concerned about the climate of the school and institution, and ask the faculty member how they are going to address the situation. The faculty member shares the incident and her class's reaction with the school leadership. The faculty member is very concerned about both the incident and the concerns expressed by students. If you were the administration, how would you respond to the faculty member and student concerns?

Discrimination on Campus

Kari Young

Basic Situation

You are the head of the diversity and inclusion team on your campus. As head of this group, your task is to promote inclusion and understanding for all races, genders, sexual orientations, and ethnicities. During the last few months, there have been flyers in the dining halls and around campus with off-color jokes about homosexuals. They are demeaning and have been getting more common as the semester goes on. In an effort to curb this behavior, you met with the head of student affairs. As a result of that meeting, a public statement was made on inclusion and diversity on the campus. Panel discussions were then held to discuss this statement.

Last night, a group of students severely beat up an openly gay student. The student was sent to the hospital and is recovering, but was badly injured. The three students who committed the crime are active on campus and generally well liked. The campus climate throughout the incidents in the dining halls has been split. Many students were fine with the jokes, and felt that certain groups needed to be less sensitive. Other students were offended, and felt as though the campus should take action against such behavior as these jokes. With this new development, you, as the public leader on campus of diversity and inclusion, must figure out what to do next. Your action plan should include what needs to be done immediately, as well as long term. Those accused of committing the crime were held over night by the local police, but are now back on campus.

Institutional Context

Your institution is a small, private liberal arts college located in a small town, but within a few hours of larger cities. It is a Catholic university affiliated with the Franciscan order. The town has always been welcoming to university students, and feels as though the campus community is a part of their community. The school has both undergraduate and graduate programs. There are approximately

2,000 undergraduates enrolled at your school, most of whom live on campus. The undergraduate student population is 85 percent Caucasian, five percent African American, three percent Asian and two percent other. Over 80 percent of the student population is Roman Catholic. The remaining percent are of various religious backgrounds. The ratio of student to faculty is 15:1. With the Catholic affiliation in mind, the institutional focus has always been on the individual. The mission includes fostering learning and promoting being a good citizen. Strength in diversity is also stated in the mission of the college, although it has been less visibly pursued by the administration in practice.

Diversity and Inclusion Team Context

Part of the creation of your administrative position came about because of students talking with administration about the lack of a welcoming atmosphere for students of different colors, sexual orientations, and religious affiliations. Your main position is as the dean of freshman on campus. You have held this position for many years and are well respected, which is why the president assigned you your new duties as the leader of the diversity and inclusion team. The student body is divided on issues of diversity, and there was a need for someone they trusted to lead an effort to change school culture surrounding this issue. The current president came to the university last year, and part of his mission is to increase diversity on campus in order to help increase enrollment. The prospective freshmen for next year are currently making decisions about where to attend. You are worried about negative press causing a decrease in enrollment.

Your Task

Please respond to the following questions:

1. How would you react the day following the events? Would you speak publicly?

2. Who would you include on your team to address this issue?

3. What action would be taken, if any, by the institution towards the students who are charged with committing the crime?

4. If the university puts out a press release or statement relating to the incident, what would it say?

5. Keeping in mind the strong religious affiliation of the campus, what would be part of your action plan to change the campus climate?

6. What leadership theories would you rely on to help lead the campus through this crisis? How could these theories help to strengthen your efforts?

Admitting and Fostering a Selective and Diverse Campus Environment

Patrick O'Neill

Basic Situation

You are the dean of undergraduate admissions at a public comprehensive college located in the northeastern United States. You report to the dean of the College of Arts and Sciences, and have a staff comprised of an assistant dean of admissions, six veteran admissions counselors, an office staff of eight, seasonal temporary workers, and a strong alumni base utilized during key times in the recruitment cycle.

Twelve years ago you were brought in to help increase the national profile and prestige of the college, which was already considered a very strong and fairly selective institution that drew most of its applicants from the Northeast. Your efforts have helped the college become known as one of the top, most selective, public, liberal arts colleges in the Northeast. Your institution now draws increasing numbers of students from other areas of the country and from abroad. You have worked hard to craft the college's national reputation as a "public ivy" institution, and to increase the student profile and rank in national publications such as *U.S. News & World Report*. During your time as dean, each year the incoming class of freshmen has seen their average SAT and GPA profile increase from 1250 to 1325 (verbal and math) and 3.52 to 3.71/4.0, respectively. National rankings have placed the college near the top of lists of public liberal arts colleges. Advancement activities have never been more successful, and young alumni giving has had a major upswing. Unfortunately, increasing racial diversity of the admitted class has not progressed as planned by the college's administration and your superiors. Retention rates for minority students are at the lowest point they have been since you began working at the school. The campus climate has been, at times, unwelcoming, at worst, hostile, for some minority students. Further, the blatantly racist actions and attitudes of some students have received negative local media attention. You have been charged to lead your staff, and to work with the dean of the College to 1) preserve the gains in national prestige and selectivity that the institution has made; 2) find ways to increase minority student recruitment and retention; and 3) foster a more inclusive, diverse campus climate.

Institutional Context

Your institution is a small public college that grants bachelor's degrees and a few master's degrees. It is located in a small northeastern town of around 10,000 residents, including the college's students, that depends heavily on the college for economic support. It is at least a one hour car ride away from a metropolitan center. Your total undergraduate enrollment is approximately 5,000, with an additional 100 graduate students. On average, you enroll 1,000 freshman students a year, but as the prestige of the college has risen, this number has been slowly increasing over the past few years. The undergraduate student population has been, and continues to be, primarily Caucasian, and from the Northeast, although the student body has begun to include more students from outside of this geographic area. Financial support from the state has been solid, despite some other state schools having funding problems. This is in large part due to the increased prestige of the college. Many new state-of-the-art facilities (science labs, dormitory suites, library, and a state-of-the-art athletic center) have been built to support the rise in reputation of the school.

Diversity and Campus Climate Context

Despite the success of your strategy to increase the college's prestige, selectivity, and class profile, the diversity of the undergraduate student body has suffered. Recruiting underrepresented and minority students that meet your other goals related to class profile and institutional prestige has proven difficult. Over the past few years, the percentage of Caucasian students in the freshman class has increased, and the percentages of African-American and Hispanic students currently rest at only three percent each, with a slightly higher percentage of Asian students. Your college is increasingly viewed by many as both a very selective, prestigious college, and one populated almost solely by White middle and upper class students. Programs you have helmed aimed at supporting the enrollment of minority students have seen very limited success. Additionally, the small percentage of minority students that do enroll have a freshman to sophomore year retention rate of 61 percent, compared with a 92 percent retention rate for Caucasian students. There are currently no admissions staff members devoted solely to minority applicants. Instead, it has been an effort shared by a number of counselors.

According to many minority students enrolled in the college, the climate on the campus has worsened in recent years. Minority students say they feel unwelcome, occasionally hear derogatory racist language, or that "eyes are always on them," while walking around campus. Minority students that leave the college before graduating cite inadequate orientation, a sense of not belonging, and hostility from Caucasian students as the driving factors in their departure. Minority students have reported that just walking across campus can be uncomfortable because they feel their every move is scrutinized by their peers. Recently, there have been examples of racist actions by students at fraternities, in the form of "ghetto parties," where Caucasian students dressed up in "thug" clothing and a few wore blackface. This event, in conjunction with some racist comments made in recent years in the student newspaper, has caused some negative local media coverage of the college. An increasing number of Caucasian students are also finding the campus climate less diverse, and cite it as the worst aspect of their college experience. Many local residents have been increasingly upset over the bad publicity for the town in the local media, and feel it does not reflect well on their community.

Your Task

The dean of the College of Arts and Sciences has increased your recruitment budget by five percent, and your financial aid budget by three percent, specifically for the recruitment and retention of qualified minority applicants. As dean of admissions, you are charged with:

1. Increasing the number of qualified minority students in each incoming class without sacrificing the prestige and selectivity you have cultivated;

2. Moreover, you and your staff need to find ways to make your college a more attractive option for minority applicants, and to find ways to work with other campus offices and departments to improve the campus climate for minority students.

You will need to answer the following questions before leading the planning sessions for the upcoming recruitment and application cycle to enroll the next freshman class:

1. What kind of strategies within the operations of the Admissions Office might be needed to further the goal of maintaining your level of prestige while increasing the number and quality of minority applicants? What guidelines should you use or not use in evaluating applications?

2. What can you do to work with other college offices to further the task of bettering the current campus climate?

3. What is the best way to spend the extra funds provided to you by the dean of the College of Arts and Sciences to further your goal of maintaining your level of prestige, while increasing the number of minority applicants? How would you specifically use these funds and for what goals? How will you measure your level of success after one, three, and five years?

4. How can you better lead the Admissions Office and represent the college in such a way that will help you to attract and enroll an increasingly diverse student body? What values and facts about the college do you need to represent to further this goal? What leadership theories apply to this situation or better inform you in crafting a plan?

National Coming Out Day Backlash at a Community College

Julie White

Basic Situation

You are a second year sociology faculty member at a community college. You have been asked by some students to serve as a faculty advisor for the GLBTQ (gay, lesbian, bisexual, transgender, queer) student club on campus, and began serving in this role in September. The students have decided to "chalk" the campus in anticipation of National Coming Out Day, held every year on October 11.

On the night of October 10, the students got together for the chalking, and wrote various statements around campus on the sidewalks, such as "Gay Pride;" "Come out, come out wherever you are;" "Be yourself;" and "I love my lesbian sister," along with GLBTQ cultural symbols such as the pink triangle and rainbows. When you get to campus the next day, you see the chalkings on campus, and notice that some of them have been defaced and turned into negative comments about GLBTQ students. When you arrive at your office, several students are waiting for you, upset about the defacements. In addition, the club president tells you that as he was walking to your office this morning, a construction worker yelled at him, "Hey, faggot!"

Institutional Context

You work at a mid-size community college in a suburban community in the Northeast, with an enrollment of 8,000 students. The college is open-access, and known for serving students from a wide variety of socioeconomic and academic backgrounds. The college has programs and services for students who are not academically prepared for college-level classes, along with a thriving honors program. The GLBTQ club has been in existence, off and on, for ten years. The racial composition of the student body is: 65 percent White; 25 percent African-American; six percent Hispanic/Latino; and four percent Other/Unknown. About 58 percent of the students are female. The average age of students is 24. While most students commute to campus from their homes, residence halls house about 200 students on campus, and nearby apartment complexes house approximately 500 students.

The Faculty/Departmental Context

The Sociology Department is known for its liberal leanings, and you were hired in part because of your background in queer theory. Other faculty have expressed supportive statements to you in regard to GLBTQ issues on campus. However, your academic dean is known to be fairly conservative in nature. While she states that she values diversity and inclusion as general principles, you detect a certain aloofness from her. She appears uncomfortable when you mention your partner in passing, and although spouses are often invited to academic functions, there is never language that states that "significant others," or "partners," are welcome, and you have never seen a same-sex couple at one of these events. Having only been at the college for the last two years, you are untenured.

Your Task

You must determine how to respond to these recent events. Specifically:

1. Who should you notify about the defacement of the chalking? What would be some applicable campus policies for this situation?

2. How can you best support the students, who are feeling violated and scared, due to both the chalking defacement, and the harassment of the club president?

3. How should you direct the club president in terms of reporting the harassment by the construction worker?

4. Are there other responses that you would recommend to campus administration, in light of these events?

Update One

Later in the same day, the vice-president for administration, who oversees grounds and facilities, calls to tell you that all chalkings will be washed off the sidewalks, including those which were not defaced. S/he informs you that the students may not replace them with new chalking. The students are upset that they have been barred from replacing the chalked messages. Meanwhile, the students have asked you to speak at that night's rally (which had been planned prior to these recent events) about the importance of inclusion. Expecting your audience to be primarily students and a few supportive faculty and staff, you plan a fiery speech advocating for full and equal rights for GLBTQ individuals. When you arrive at the rally, the students tell you that they invited the vice-president of the college to attend, and s/he should be there at any moment.

1. What do you say to the vice-president? Do you react to his/her statement? If so, how? If not, why not?

2. How do you advise the students to proceed? Do you encourage them to advocate replacing the chalking? Why or why not?

3. Does the fact that the vice-president will be there change your speech? Why or why not?

Update Two

The rally goes off fine, and although the vice-president seems somewhat uncomfortable, you do not receive any negative feedback. The next day, several faculty and staff come to you and express their desire to do more for GLBTQ inclusion on campus. They tell you that in light of this week's events, they would like to do something visible to show their support.

1. How do you direct the faculty and staff? What is your approach to their desire to do something?

2. What resources could you draw on to promote a more inclusive campus for GLBTQ students? How much energy would you put into ongoing efforts in this arena? Do your interactions with your dean, and/or the fact that you are untenured, affect your decision about your level of ongoing involvement and advocacy for GLBTQ students?

Strategic Planning for an Academic Program

Andrew Wall

Basic Situation

You are a group of faculty from a higher education graduate program within a school of education at a private research university in the northeastern United States. Your graduate program has undergone a near total transformation in the past five years. Five years ago, a program review was completed for your program, and a basic strategic plan was developed. The strategic plan called for the transition of the program from an esoteric, disciplinary focused, degree program with fewer than 50 students, to a more practically oriented degree program that might better serve the needs of those students interested in higher education graduate degrees. The program review and related strategic outline for action called for some of the following strategic steps and related actions:

1. Recruit new faculty who have a strong academic preparation in the degree area of higher education or student affairs, with related professional experience. In the past three years three new tenure-track faculty have been hired with this exact profile;

2. Revise the program curriculum to be up to date with peer programs in higher education across the country. There was a major curriculum reinvigoration completed two years ago;

3. Raise enrollment in the program through directed marketing of the new program and faculty, and the creation of an accelerated Ed.D. program. The formation of the accelerated Ed.D. program was completed three years ago and today enrolls between 10-15 new Ed.D. accelerated students each year. The program has also grown from about 40 students five years ago, to nearly 110 students today;

4. Improve the program graduation rate from hovering in the mid-30 percent range. This goal has also begun to be improved with a graduate rate over the past two to three years moving toward 60 percent;

5. Raise the profile of the program nationally through research productivity and doctoral student achievement. This goal has seen significant accomplishment with one of the faculty earning a national early career research award, and a Ph.D. student earning a national dissertation fellowship to support her project;

6. Improve the local reputation of the higher education program. The program review revealed that the broader university, or regional higher education community, perceived the program in a poor light. There has been significant anecdotal evidence that perception of the program has shifted to the positive.

Institutional Context

Despite these positive developments, there are significant challenges facing the higher education program as it moves into a new five-year strategic planning horizon. Issues of concern include:

1. Lack of financial support for graduate students. Support that is lacking relates to graduate assistantships at both the master's and doctoral levels;

2. Comparatively high tuition price and net cost compared to peer programs that are regionally competitive;

3. A curriculum that is not in 100 percent compliance with Council of Academic Standards (CAS) guidelines, the professional higher education program guidelines;

4. High student to faculty advising ratio, particularly when considering the number of Ed.D. and Ph.D. students to faculty (15:1);

5. A junior faculty (all tenure track faculty are assistant professors);

6. A concern expressed by some students that there is not a clear higher education program community. There has been a well articulated desire for the faculty to develop one;

7. There is ever-present concern over enrollment and ensuring a diverse and talented student population within the program. In particular, student writing and doctoral student research preparation are areas of concern for the faculty as they look to program enhancement; and finally,

8. Unknown quality of program graduates, though the program believes them to be excellently prepared.

Your Task

You and your team have been asked to provide a starting point for the development of a strategic plan for the program. Your team happens to have unique insider knowledge of this graduate program, and as such is able to apply your knowledge to the development of a set of strategic planning information for consideration by the faculty and administration.

Your challenge is to respond to the following set of tasks in the development of a strategic plan. Please write up your recommendations for action so that they might be submitted for consideration by the graduate program faculty.

1. Using your unique knowledge, identify the student needs and desires for the graduate program;

2. Develop a set of questions related to the program to be answered by the faculty of the program;

3. Develop a set of recommendations for program development (change) of the higher education program;

4. Identify who has power and influence related to the graduate program. How do issues of power and influence impact how you might think about recommendations for change or program evolution? What role does leadership have in program development?

Creation of a New Staffing Position

Jenna Dell

Basic Situation

You are a senior administrator at a small, private institution located in the northeastern United States. Along with the other deans and selected faculty members and students, you will be responsible for creating and staffing a new dean position for study abroad and interdepartmental studies. This person will work closely with the international student director and under the dean of Student Life. Based on the job description below, you will be responsible for identifying qualities that the director should have, considering and incorporating what students, faculty, other administrators have indicated they desire in such a candidate. Additionally, you will create a strategic plan to accomplish goals that the director should reach based on the institutional goals listed.

Institutional Context

Your institution is a small, private institution that primarily grants bachelor's degrees. A small number of master's degrees in education and management are also offered. Undergraduate enrollment is approximately 1,200 full-time students, 90 percent of whom are undergraduates that live on campus. Approximately 13 percent of the students are from foreign countries, and 35 countries are represented in the undergraduate population. As a private college, the institution relies primarily on tuition and its endowment. Though the college is not considered very prestigious, in 2006 it was awarded the Triennial Award for the most outstanding Phi Beta Kappa chapter at a liberal arts college.

College Administration Context

Due to the college's size, there is a small number of senior officials. The deans of Academic Affairs, Student Affairs, Admissions, Administration, Development, and Alumni report directly to the president. Some are vice-presidents in addition to their role as dean, but there are no additional organizational divisions.

Currently, there is an international student director who is a resource to international students while they are on campus. This individual also works closely with the admissions team to ensure a smooth transition onto campus for international students arriving from their home countries. The majority of foreign students on campus are Japanese. The institution has a sister school in Sapporo called Hokusei Gakuen, and keeps close contact with other high schools in Osaka and Kobe. Additionally, each year approximately 20 students from the girl's school affiliated with Hokusei Gakuen come for an intensive ESL summer program.

In addition to foreign students attending the college, approximately 42 percent of students study abroad at some point during their four years. The associate dean of faculty currently oversees the study abroad programs. He oversees both the faculty members who take students on trips, and the Junior Year Abroad Program. In his role as associate dean, he has a large number of responsibilities beyond study abroad. Unfortunately, the associate dean does not have the time to focus greater attention on the study abroad program. As a result of this, and the struggling economy, the program has suffered. Nevertheless, enrollment continues to be high, and each year 50 percent or more of the alumni make contributions to the annual fund of the college, specifically for the study abroad program. (The college is among the top one percent in the nation in the percentage of alumni giving.)

In this new position, the study abroad director will be responsible for creating new partnerships with colleges and universities in other countries to facilitate more student exchange programs. This individual will be charged with capacity mapping for study abroad expansion, including non-traditional destinations in Asia, Africa, and Latin America. The new director must work to engage faculty to take more trips, and to revamp their curriculum to incorporate educational goals in trips abroad. Finally, and possibly the most challenging, the individual must come up with ways in which these goals can be met financially, despite a struggling economy.

Your Task

Your first step is to:

1. Identify what qualities as a leader this person should have, whether they be an individual's behaviors, traits, style of leadership, or a combination of all three. Remember that this

person will work closely with other administrators, students, and faculty members who take the students on trips;

2. Determine how you will conduct this staff member search; and finally

3. Identify how the person will go about accomplishing the institutional goals by implementing different styles of leadership.

Unionization and Collective Bargaining: Non-Tenure Track Adjunct Faculty

J.B. Rodgers

Basic Situation

You and your group are non-tenure track adjunct faculty members at a small, private liberal arts institution in the Northeast. Working as a representative group for your other non-tenure track adjunct teaching faculty colleagues, you are working with the administration to organize an election to see what number of the institution's 450 adjuncts would agree to be represented by the Lecturer's Employee Organization (LEO), an affiliate of the American Federation of Teachers (AFT). Membership in the LEO would give non-tenure track adjunct faculty collective bargaining rights when negotiating future contracts with the institution.

Institutional Context

With a growing number of students at your institution, adjunct faculty have been bridging the gap between a limited amount of funding for full-time tenure track faculty positions, and the need for more teaching faculty to fill the void left by full-time tenure track faculty increasingly immersed in research obligations. Adjunct faculty at your institution are considered "at-will" employees, and must renew their contracts each and every semester. Adjunct faculty have no access to the employment benefits normally provided by the institution. This includes health and dental insurance, participation in the intuition's 403(b) retirement fund, and tuition benefits for further education. Also, adjunct faculty cannot access research and travel funding, and exist outside the scope of faculty governance. Furthermore, adjunct faculty do not qualify to utilize the collective bargaining units existing at the institution for full-time tenure track faculty.

The only other employees who are currently unionized at your institution are the service workers. They are organized with the Service Employees International Union (SEIU). The administration is opposed to allowing adjuncts to unionize, and they have indicated that they are in a position to terminate at-will employees' contracts at any time based on the need for their services. However, they have agreed to allow you and your group to organize the election to ascertain the percentage of adjuncts that wish to unionize. For the most part, full-time tenure track faculty are also opposed to the idea. They see the increased amount of non-tenure track faculty, who work for significantly less money, as a threat to their positions in the long term, as the funding for any increases in the pay or benefits packages for adjuncts must come from somewhere.

Legal Context

For the most part, established higher education legal precedent has been a double-edged sword. On the one hand, the courts have not usually viewed adjunct faculty as a collective body in the same way that they would view tenured faculty. On the other hand, the courts normally consider unionization cases on an individual basis, and put emphasis on the contextualization of the case through institution-specific facts. From a legal perspective, the most important thing to keep in mind is that the success of a case involving the ability to organize and collectively bargain often lies in the court's perception of the adjunct as a self-employed individual, or as a worker within the institutional system. If the court sees the adjunct as a worker, they will be more inclined to rule in favor of their ability to organize and collectively bargain.

Your Task

You and your group are going ahead with the election. Assuming that you get a majority of responses saying "yes" to organizing with LEO, as the responsible party, you need to consider the following scenarios and the possible ramifications of each:

1. The administration has agreed to meet with your group to discuss possible changes to the current contractual system. However, they have indicated that due to the "at-will" status of adjuncts, the contracts can be terminated at anytime. What issues will you focus on from the standpoint of the contract? Is it better to focus on fighting for longer-term contracts, or better to focus on benefits and pay rates? Would you want to focus on both?

2. The board of trustees has indicated to the administration that they will not recognize the results of the election. Drawing on

higher education law precedent, what recourse does your group have in the courts? What ramifications will this have in the event that employment for adjuncts at your institution is threatened?

3. Tenure-track faculty at your institution are organizing a protest. They are lobbying the board of trustees and the administration to not allow adjuncts to organize. What possible avenues could you pursue to form alliances with the tenure-track faculty? Do you stage a counter-protest? What concerns of the tenure-track faculty need to be addressed, when framing the narrative surrounding adjunct faculty unionization and collective bargaining rights?

4. Identify your leadership approach to organizing for a vote on being represented by a union.

Leadership Challenges in Higher Education Related to Gender Career Fear

Kristen Emery

The Situation

You are a tenured faculty member at Willmott University, a private, medium-sized research university in the northeastern United States. You have worked at Willmott University for several decades in student affairs, and are now a full-time, tenured professor in the higher education program at the Thoms School of Education at Willmott University.

You have many advisees in the Ph.D. program in higher education at the Thoms School, and recently, three of your female advisees requested a joint meeting with you. In the meeting, they described an alarming situation in which Dr. Hill, a male tenured senior professor in the higher education program, repeatedly made derogatory comments to the members of his doctoral level classes stating that "female faculty hardly ever gain tenure," and "the pursuit of a career as a faculty member at a research institution is a waste of time for any woman seeking both tenure and a family in today's world." Dr. Hill has also hinted that women in his classes who hope to teach at a college or university will likely be unsuccessful in their fields if they already have children.

When you ask your three female advisees why they did not come to you sooner, they state that they enjoy Dr. Hill's classes, admire his research, and had hoped to assist him with projects relating to a new widely anticipated textbook that he is currently writing. They, and you, are aware that Dr. Hill is known worldwide for his research, commitment to service and higher education, and for the large research and scholarship grants that he brings to Willmott each year.

Your three advisees had collectively decided to ignore Dr. Hill's comments in class, but have now come to the conclusion that they would like someone from the Thoms School to speak with him. In addition, your advisees voice that while they would like someone to talk with Dr. Hill about the effects of his words (and they would prefer not to speak to him directly), more than anything, they are deeply concerned about the validity of his statements, as they are all within months of graduation, have children, and plan on pursuing full-time faculty positions in higher education at major research institutions.

Institutional Context

Willmott University enrolls students in bachelor's, master's, and doctoral programs. Willmott has an enrollment of 15,008 students with 10,002 full-time undergraduates, 983 evening full and part-time undergraduates, and 4,023 full and part-time graduate students. Of the 4,023 graduate students, most are in law, business, and arts and sciences graduate programs. Currently, the Thoms School of Education has 1,600 enrolled students. Each year the school receives 1,100 applications and admits only 260 students (24%).

Willmott has 675 full-time faculty, of which only 262 (39%) are female. Willmott has a 1:12 faculty-student ratio and 97 percent of Willmott faculty have doctoral degrees.

The Thoms School of Education has 54 full-time faculty members, 28 part-time faculty members, 600 undergraduate students, 1,000 graduate students, and more than 25 academic programs in education, human development, and psychology. The school is large, highly competitive, innovative, and places strong emphasis on diversity in admissions, community and campus efforts, and student, staff, faculty, and administrative awareness.

Your Task

With their permission, after your meeting with your three female student advisees, you immediately schedule a meeting with the dean of the Thoms school. You are concerned that Dr. Hill (whom you know only on a professional level, if that) has made such discouraging comments to graduate students at the Thoms school. After your meeting, you suspect that the dean will, as she has in the past, request that you put a task force together to manage student concerns relating to these issues. With this knowledge, you begin to analyze how you will organize this initiative and its challenges, as you navigate the following:

1. You met with the dean and explained the situation that your three female Ph.D. students relayed to you. The dean stated that she will personally talk with Dr. Hill, but first has

requested that, if possible, you provide her with documentation from your advisees about the several instances in which inappropriate comments were made. You must meet with your students again and request this from them. As this is a sensitive issue, and they are quite upset with Dr. Hill and the Thoms School in general, what leadership approach will you use when you talk with your advisees about the dean's request?

2. You, the three graduate student advisees, and the dean, are all well aware that Dr. Hill has just won an American Educational Research Association (AERA) award honoring him for his substantial research accomplishments and excellence in the field of higher education. University media have been interviewing Dr. Hill all week, and an article about his award is presently on the main page of Willmott's website. How will this information and the fact that Dr. Hill is a symbol for Willmott, as well as for the Thoms School, effect this situation? Who has power and influence in this situation?

3. The dean has asked you and several other faculty members to put together a task force aimed at researching post-degree women in higher education careers, and female tenured faculty in the United States with families. The dean has also asked the task force to research Thoms graduate student career counseling and guidance for female graduate students. While technically, you (and the other faculty members) are not obligated to participate in this task-force, your advisees' concern has inspired you, and you believe you may be able to incorporate the experience into some of your current research. From here, the task force must:

   a. Gather and prepare information on post-degree women in higher education careers, and female tenured faculty in the United States with families. How can this information be presented to students?

   b. Consider what Willmott is presently doing and could be doing to promote and encourage institutional diversity and, more specifically, gender inclusion (i.e. clubs, campus and community events, curriculum, etc.).

c. Identify graduate student needs for the Thoms School, providing information on career options, career counseling, and work-life balance management to its students. What role should faculty and students have in this?

April Fools or Foes

Liz Bremer

Basic Situation

The student newspaper has just released their annual April Fools edition. Traditionally, the paper has been filled with comedic spoofs and satire pieces regarding various aspects of campus and university life. However, this year's edition had gone too far. The front page featured two controversial stories. The leading story reported that members of the Renaissance Club—a well respected student club on campus notorious for its weekly recreation sessions on Tuesday nights outside the library—had attacked a group of Chinese graduate students heading back to their residences located next to the library. It was reported that at least two students were hospitalized, and that another dozen were injured. The club members' "weapons" had been confiscated, and campus police were investigating the incident.

The second story featured the women's soccer coach. The coach, who also coordinated the intramural program, was allegedly arrested on domestic violence charges. It was also revealed that there were a number of sexual harassment charges from students being looked into, and that the coach had similar issues at the institution where s/he had previously worked. In addition, the paper featured a number of articles with crude and vulgar language, and a political cartoon featuring one of the school's highly regarded philosophy professors acting as an advisor to a militant secret society while the dean looked the other way (secret societies were banned at the university in the mid-twentieth century).

Institutional Context

The institution is a large public research university that offers undergraduate, graduate, and professional degree programs. The university also boasts a highly reputable athletic program. There is an undergraduate enrollment of 21,000 and a graduate enrollment of 8,000, over a total of nine campuses. The main campus has close to 17,000 undergraduate students, of which 70 percent of these students live on campus; 20 percent are minority students, and one percent is international students. The average SAT score for incoming students is about 1200, with a one-year retention rate of 93 percent, and a six-year graduation rate of 76 percent.

The past several months have been difficult for the institution. The university has been experiencing significant budget cuts in light of a major state deficit. Individual colleges and programs have been asked to make large cuts. For example, all core mathematics classes are now being taught in lectures with 100 students by a faculty member. Previously, these classes were taught in 25-30 person sections by a teaching assistant, and courses were coordinated by a faculty member. This specific change increases class size, and decreases aid to graduate students. Similar actions can be seen in all the departments throughout the university.

The student newspaper is published Monday through Friday, and has been publishing daily (through the academic year) for over 50 years. Ten thousand copies of the paper are delivered to 80 different pick up locations on the main campus, one of the satellite campuses, and in the local community. The staff consists of approximately 120 students, and uses top technology to print the news. The newspaper has been operating independently from the organized student government for the past 40 years.

Your Task

You are the president of the university. You have only been in office since June, so this is your first experience with the April Fools edition of the newspaper at this institution. You have received a number of phone calls pertaining to the paper. The directors of Residential Life and the Graduate School have called reporting that they have international students who are concerned for their safety, not realizing that the newspaper was a gag edition. Members of the board and representatives from the NCAA are irate that a highly regarded public figure—the soccer coach— has become the brunt of a very bad joke. The subjects of all these pieces are offended and outraged, and the overall student response to the edition has been very unreceptive.

Please respond to the following questions:

1. What is your immediate response? What is your long term strategy?

2. What leadership traits/behaviors will you utilize?

3. What leadership approach, along with specific behaviors, will you utilize in addressing this situation?

4. What are possible ways to resolve this situation, and what risks are present for you and the institution?

Institutional Alcohol Policy

Lisabeth Tinelli

Basic Situation

You have been president of a four year public liberal arts university in the northeastern United States for thirteen years. Previously, you served as the institution's provost and interim president. A substantial portion of your work as president has been to develop specific strategies to increase student involvement within the community, with a specific focus on addressing and linking on-campus and community needs and issues. Part of the strategic plan has been to develop partnerships with other leading public colleges and community institutions. Toward this end, you are the director of the local Chamber of Commerce, and serve on the board of directors for the Center for Governmental Research.

Institutional Context

Your public liberal arts institution offers 48 undergraduate degrees. The student population is approximately 5,000, with a student/faculty ratio of 17:1. Recently, the undergraduate college proclaimed itself an "honor's college," establishing its distinction as a small liberal arts college with highly selective admissions, small class sizes, and student-centered teaching focus. In 2008, *Kiplinger's Personal Finance* listed your college as the number one "Best Value Public College" in the nation for out-of-state students, and number six in the nation for in-state residents. As a state school, *US News & Report* identified your institution as a "best buy" among public schools, and lauded it for its academic programs, accessible professors, and hometown atmosphere.

The university offers a wide range of diverse organizations and activities, including several local and Greek organizations, including eight fraternities and ten sororities. The university is also home to several off-campus organizations that serve as alternatives to Greek life. One such organization, the Orange Knights, was banished from campus in 1996 after two students were hospitalized for excessive drinking, but continues to function as an off-campus club. Most recently, a sophomore student from your university participated in a two-day drinking initiation hosted by the Orange Knights that resulted in the student's death at the house of other club members. The party consisted mainly of university students, and was hosted outdoors on a street adjacent to the university for over six hours.

Prior to the student's death, local police were contacted the evening of the party by an on-campus residence employee who voiced safety concerns for the students present. By the time a village police officer arrived at the scene, the party had dissipated, and observing no one outside, the police officer left without entering the house. A few news reports have indicated that a university student may have "tipped-off" members of the organization to warn them of the imminent arrival of the police, giving party goers enough time to move inside. The following morning, police were notified via 911 by residents of the house of the student's death.

An investigation is being conducted to determine the parties responsible for the young man's death. Two university students, and one local resident, have been charged with criminally negligent homicide, in addition to unlawfully dealing with a child, criminal nuisance, and first and second degree hazing. One student has been charged with tampering with physical evidence, as he allegedly removed the organization's jersey from the student's body before the police arrived.

Your Task

You have been asked to develop a strategic plan to address the college's alcohol drinking policy. A position paper was produced by the vice-president of the college in 2004, and is posted on the college website, albeit in an obscure location. Otherwise, the drinking policy for your college, formal or informal, is ambiguous at best. Your task is to respond to the following questions and issues:

1. Identify the problems facing the university.

2. What type of leadership approach will you use to guide your actions in response to this situation, and in crafting an institutional response to the college student drinking?

3. What are your major leadership responsibilities in this situation?

4. What role does leadership have in developing an alcohol policy?

5. Develop a set of recommendations for the development of an official alcohol policy.

6. How do issues of power and influence impact how you might think about recommendations for change or program evolution?

Love in the College Setting

Karen Taylor

Basic Situation

Due to a recent outcry from the student government, Little Bear Creek Community College has just instituted a strict policy of no fraternization between faculty and students. In the past five years there have been four incidents of faculty members and students dating each other. The student government has brought this issue to the attention of the Faculty Senate, and the senate passed the policy which the president and the Board of Trustees have signed.

John and Mary have been dating for one year. John has just been laid off from his job, and the state will pay for retraining if he attends the local community college (Little Bear Creek Community College). Mary has just been hired as an adjunct instructor to teach paralegal courses at the same college. John is a computer repair major, and will never have to take any courses from Mary. A member of the board sees John and Mary out socially one weekend, and on Monday morning calls the president to inform him of this breach of policy, and to insist that Mary be fired. Mary was not informed of this policy when she was hired.

Institutional Context

Little Bear Creek Community College is located in the Midwest. It grants 63 associate degrees and certificates. Full-time students number just over 3,000, while part-time students hover above 3,500. There are currently 100 full time faculty, and 200 adjunct faculty members. The average class size is 18, with a student to teacher ratio of 16:1. The average age of the students is 28, with females outnumbering males two to one.

Little Bear Creek Community College has an open door policy for admission. In-state students pay $2,500 per year, and out of state students pay $3,000 per year in tuition. Ninety-two percent of the full-time students receive some form of financial aid. Ninety-one percent of the recent graduates are either employed or have transferred to a four year institution.

Another draw to Little Bear Creek Community College is the housing that is available to students that is within walking distance of the campus. Students can rent apartment style housing with four students per apartment. Cable, phone, high speed internet, laundry, and all utilities are included in the rent of $4,000 per academic year. There are spaces for 350 students.

Student Government/Faculty Academic Senate Context

The student government and the faculty senate have had a long history of supporting each other in college matters. In the past, the faculty senate supported the students in their request for a plus/minus system to be added to the grading system, and the students supported the faculty in their request for mandatory advisement before registration. Thus, when the student government began to field complaints from the student body regarding fraternization between students and faculty, the student government asked and received support from the faculty senate.

Your Task

Your challenge is to respond to the following questions and complete the requested tasks:

1. Should the president of Little Bear Creek Community College fire Mary? Why or why not?

2. When should the college have mentioned this new policy? In the interview with Mary, or even before the interview on the employment application?

3. Does an employer have the right to interfere in one's personal life outside of the workplace? Why or Why not?

Revising the Current Student Affairs Model

Chris Grant

Basic Situation

You are a committee of faculty and administrators from a large public institution. Recently, it has been noted that the undergraduate population has grown too large for the current student affairs model to support it. There has been an increase in on-campus parties, underage drinking, and drug related offenses. Residential housing has continued to become increasingly unruly, despite the best efforts of the staff to maintain an appropriate environment. Academic and cultural clubs are seen as having racial boundaries, and pockets of segregation have formed. Due to noise and property damage, community relations with the surrounding neighbors are in serious decline. Connections between classroom work and extra-curricular activities are few and far between, and the quality of learning and related reputation of the institution is starting to suffer. Faculty are feeling frustrated because the work that they do in the classroom is not being supported by the campus at large. Student affairs administrators are struggling to serve an ever-growing student body with limited financial resources and manpower. In short, a holistic learning environment is lacking on campus.

Institutional Context

There are a total of 42,367 students enrolled at your institution, with 8,943 undergraduates living in residential housing. The institution has a total of 30 residence halls, divided into three distinct clusters throughout the campus. Degrees are offered through the doctoral level, and there is a student to faculty ratio of 21:1. Students take part in 353 different clubs and activities, and there are 60 recognized fraternities and sororities. Approximately 15 percent of the students are part of a historically underrepresented minority group, and the campus is almost evenly divided between male and female students.

Your Task

The president is unhappy with the current trend in student affairs, and fears that if something is not done, the reputation of the institution will be damaged. Minor steps taken in the past have not worked, and it has become apparent that now is the time for a complete overhaul of the existing framework. Academic endeavors in the classroom can no longer be negatively impacted by a loosely structured extracurricular system. Your committee is tasked with 1) evaluating the current student affairs model, and 2) detailing a plan to shift from the current approach to a more progressive model. The committee will need to have a holistic focus on all aspects of student development, and determine methods of incorporating classroom work into extra-curricular activities. It will be necessary to work closely with both faculty and administration in order to develop a system both groups will feel comfortable implementing. While this will be a difficult undertaking, it cannot be avoided. Keep in mind the following questions as you work:

1. What are the key elements that will need to change in order to make a new model operate effectively?

2. In what ways can academic and student affairs administrators work together that are not currently being utilized?

3. What will be your process for gathering relevant data on the current model, as well as similar models at peer institutions?

4. Which theories, or approach to leadership, will be most effective in implementing the shift from the old model to the new one?

5. What impact will the current economic climate have on implementing your new model?

Leadership Challenges in Facing Financial Tensions

Andrew Wall

Basic Situation

You are the dean of liberal arts and sciences at a small-liberal arts institution located in the Midwest. You have been at the institution for two years, and in general you feel as though you know the faculty, staff and students. The informal and formal feedback you have received has been positive. Due to the recent downturn in the national economy, the institution's president has asked for you to plan for three different budget scenarios for the coming year:

1. a flat (zero growth in budget year);

2. a three percent reduction in your budget; and

3. a six percent reduction in your budget.

Institutional Context

Historically, your institution is loosely affiliated with the Methodist Church. The institution was founded in 1856 by a group of Methodist clergy and parishioners with the idea of providing a good education to those living on the prairie of the Midwest. The institution now boasts an enrollment of 2,200 undergraduate students, with an additional continuing education program that has a yearly enrollment of 1,200 students in degree and non-degree programs. The institution has four colleges: liberal arts and sciences; business; education; and continuing education, and is located in a city of 45,000 people in the state of Illinois. The school is the major employer of the city, and an economic engine for regional economic vitality.

The reputation of the institution is solid, as are the students who enter the institution. Last year, the average entering first year student had an ACT score of 24.29, making it the strongest class in the past five years (there were 550 entering freshmen). The school recently launched a significant marketing campaign to brand the college as a first choice institution for those seeking a religiously affiliated private liberal arts student experience. While the institution recruits nationally, most of the students at the institution are from Illinois, with over 60 percent of enrolled students from within a 100-mile radius of the campus. Though the institution has strived to diversify the student body, it is still overwhelmingly Caucasian (84%) and of traditional age (nearly 98%). Among other ethnic groups, there are about five percent African American and eight percent Latino/a.

The institution has worked diligently over the past twenty years to build its endowment and infrastructure. Recent years have seen the successful completion of a new student center and two academic buildings. In general, the campus buildings and infrastructure are in good repair, but a major project is planned to update the institutions power grid that is anticipated to cost 25 million dollars over the next three budget years. The endowment has grown dramatically in the past 20 years from roughly 10 million dollars in 1990, to almost 100 million at the beginning of this academic year. However, one of the big institutional challenges is that with the economic downturn, the endowment has lost nearly 29 percent of its value since October. The institution has worked hard to keep its tuition cost under control, and currently charges $22,000 in tuition and fees for full-time enrollment plus $7,200 for room and board. The student discount rate is about 42 percent, or the average student pays 58 percent of the posted $22,000 tuition and fee cost.

The College of Liberal Arts and Sciences Context

The College of Liberal Arts and Sciences is the largest college at the institution with 1,200 full-time student majors, and 110 faculty and staff. There are 68 tenured or tenure track faculty members, 17 full-time clinical faculty, and 28 academic administrative staff. Within the College, there are six different departments, each with a department chair. The different departments often view themselves in competition for institutional resources, just as the College of Liberal Arts and Sciences views itself in competition with the three other colleges for resources. The mission of the College of Liberal Arts and Sciences has been to provide a strong liberal arts education that is rooted in academic disciplines. Recently, this approach has come under scrutiny by students, alumni and employers, as they worry about how a traditional liberal arts education is preparing them for the workforce.

When you were hired as dean, you were asked to review and update the curriculum to be cutting edge for the twenty-first century, and to expand institutional student quality and enrollment by 50-100 students per class. Your efforts to review and update the curriculum are under way, but have not yet resulted in realized organizational change. Similarly, your faculty is graying, with 35 of the 68 tenured or tenure track faculty within 5 years of retirement age. One of your specific aims has been to revitalize the faculty of your institution to ensure the human resources to maintain the high-quality learning experience that has been a hallmark of the College of Liberal Arts and Sciences.

Your Task

You and your administrative team have had to put all challenges and agenda items in the context of the recent national economic picture. With a major change in endowment, it can be anticipated that the endowment income will be dramatically decreased. Historically, the endowment has been drawn at a six percent rate, so it was anticipated that the institution would have $6,000,000 in endowment revenue during the coming academic year. With the drop in endowment value, this figure could be only $4,200,000, or 30 percent less than originally planned. Additionally, there is mounting evidence that students are facing new financial hardships in attending your institution. You have already had three students take leaves of absence due to changes in their parents' ability to provide financial support for their tuition and fees. Overall, the institution is facing a tough immediate financial future, hence the president's call for budget planning scenarios of flat or three to six percent decreases in spending. Your challenge is to examine the following questions as you plan for your next budget cycle:

1. How do you think about the role of leadership in making the current budget planning decisions? What approaches to leadership seem to be most applicable in this situation?

2. Develop a leadership plan for addressing this budget planning case that utilizes what you have read about leadership to date. What will be your approach, who will you include in the process, and why?

3. What will the role of values and mission be in making decisions in the case scenario?

4. How will you think about your overall leadership agenda in light of the recent financial challenges?

5. By what process will you determine your coming year academic budget?

Contributor Biographies

Chelsea BaileyShea is a research associate and postdoctoral fellow at the Warner Center. She currently works on program evaluation projects at the Center, as well as collaborates with a research team led by Andrew Wall. Her research interests include women in higher education, institutional support for student success, and issues surrounding college student participation in study abroad.

Jenna Dell is an Ed.D. student in higher education administration at the Warner School of Education where she received her M.S. in 2010. She received her B.S. in anthropology and sociology from Elmira College in 2007. Her research interests include the effect participation in study abroad programs has on culture capital and college student development. Dell received the Walter I. Garms Award for Educational Leadership in 2010.

Michael Edelman is a current student at the Warner School of Education. His primary research interests have been in the areas of access and retention in higher education. While he is currently working in the field of mental health, he is interested in pursuing his career in student affairs upon his graduation in May of 2011.

Kristen L. Emery is a Ph.D. student in higher education at the Warner School of Education. Emery completed her M.S. in business service management from the Rochester Institute of Technology. Prior to pursuing her doctoral work, she worked as an admissions and financial aid officer at the Graduate School of Arts and Sciences at Harvard University. Emery is presently working on her dissertation, and aims to explore the intersection of gender, tenure, and faculty work-life balance at research-extensive universities in the northeastern United States. Emery is also an adjunct instructor for Finger Lakes Community College, and a teaching assistant in the business program at Harvard University. Her primary areas of interest include academic leadership and entrepreneurialism, gender and parenting studies, faculty work-life balance management, and academic tenure.

Christopher Grant has been working in higher education for close to ten years, starting his career in residential life. Presently, he works for a program designed to increase access for low income, first-generation, and under-represented minority students. While currently taking time off for his family, he hopes to return to school soon with the ultimate goal of earning a Ph.D. in higher education.

Nahoko Kawakyu O'Connor is a doctoral student in higher education at the Warner School of Education. She takes a sociological approach to examining power relations in society, with a specific focus in higher education. Her research interests include federal financial aid policy, purpose of higher education, and theories of social stratification. She likes to cook, eat, and feed others.

Michael Mestan has a bachelor's degree in human anatomy and is a Doctor of Chiropractic. He has worked as a general chiropractor, served as chief resident during his residency, and began a specialty radiology consultation practice. Mestan served on the executive committee of the American Chiropractic College of Radiology for six years, as well as has been a faculty member at Parker College of Chiropractic and the New York Chiropractic College. He is currently the executive vice-president and provost at the New York Chiropractic College, and attends the Warner School of Education studying higher education leadership. His research interests include entrepreneurialism in higher education and governance associated with leadership teams.

Patrick O'Neill is an admissions counselor at the University of Rochester, and a 2010 graduate of the Warner School of Education with an M.S. in higher education administration. His research focused on new nonprofit groups dedicated to increasing access to selective higher education institutions for underrepresented students. O'Neill did his undergraduate work in history and Africana studies at Fordham University and SUNY Geneseo. He came to Admissions at the University in 2007, after years of working as a public library supervisor.

Joseph Parker is an assistant director of information technology at the University of Rochester. He received his B.A. from SUNY Geneseo, and has been involved in many areas of information technology including operations, infrastructure, data warehousing and application development. His current responsibilities include support and development of student administrative systems.

Joseph W. Rodgers is a Ph.D. student at the Warner School of Education. His research areas include assessment practice, community involvement, and higher education as it relates to the public good.

Michelle L. Rogers is the assistant deputy to the president at the University of Rochester. In her current role, she directs operations for the Office of the President, oversees presidential events, and conducts special projects in support of institutional priorities. Rogers joined the University of Rochester in 2004 as the assistant director of IT Communications, bringing with her 10 years of IT publishing and marketing experience. Rogers is enrolled in the educational leadership program at the Warner School of Education, with an anticipated completion of the M.S in higher education administration in May 2011. Her research interests include college access for rural students, the cost structure of higher education, and faculty development.

Karen Taylor is currently the associate dean of records and advisement at Genesee Community College. She is in her third year of the accelerated Ed.D. higher education administration program at the Warner School of Education. Taylor has spent twenty-seven years in the field of education in the public school system and higher education in teaching and administration. Her current research interests are in the field of academic assessment. She has an M.S. in Education/TESOL from Nazareth College in Rochester and a B.S. in English from Utah State University.

Lisabeth Tinelli is a Ph.D. student at the Warner School of Education. Her research focuses on the functions of social theory in literacy learning, in particular an analysis of the multiliteracies of youth. She currently teaches a literacy education theories course, and an academic writing course that engages students in critical literacy as a means to enact social change.

Rudy Trejo currently serves as teen leadership program director for the YWCA El Paso del Norte Region. He graduated from St. Edward's University with a degree in political science in 2008, and will be obtaining his master's degree in educational administration with an emphasis in student affairs from the University of Texas at El Paso in May 2011. His research interest includes understanding the greater impact student involvement plays in the development of college students, student leadership assessment, and minority affairs.

Andrew F. Wall is an assistant professor of higher education at the Warner School of Education. His research examines college student health and learning, assessment and evaluation in higher education, state educational finance, and public trust in education.

Julie White is an advanced doctoral student at the Warner School of Education. She is currently the assistant director of student services and assistant professor at Monroe Community College. Her research interests include community colleges, policy effects on students (with a particular focus on financial aid and welfare legislation), and student health issues.

Kari A. Young is an administrator at the University of Rochester, where she has worked for the last five years. She received her B.A. from SUNY Geneseo, and her M.S. from the Warner School of Education. Her research interests include adult learners and military veterans returning to higher education.

CPSIA information can be obtained
at www.ICGtesting.com
Printed in the USA
LVOW12s0543090817

544334LV00001B/11/P

9 781458 327598